THE IMAGINARY INVALID

Molière
Translated by
Richard Nelson,
Richard Pevear, and
Larissa Volokhonsky

BROADWAY PLAY PUBLISHING INC
New York
www.broadwayplaypub.com
info@broadwayplaypub.com

THE IMAGINARY INVALID
© Copyright 2021 Richard Nelson, Richard Pevear, &
Larissa Volokhonsky

First edition: June 2021
I S B N: 978-0-88145-836-7

Book design: Marie Donovan
Page make-up: Adobe InDesign
Typeface: Palatino

THE IMAGINARY INVALID was first produced 10 February 1673 at the Théâtre du Palais-Royal in Paris.

CHARACTERS

ARGAN, *the imaginary invalid*
BÉLINE, ARGAN's *second wife*
ANGÉLIQUE, ARGAN's *daughter*
LOUISON, ARGAN's *little daughter,* ANGÉLIQUE's *sister*
BÉRALDE, ARGAN's *brother*
CLÉANTE, *suitor of* ANGÉLIQUE
MONSIEUR DIAFOIRUS, *a doctor*
THOMAS DIAFOIRUS, *his son, suitor of* ANGÉLIQUE
MONSIEUR PURGON, ARGAN's *doctor*
MONSIEUR FLEURANT, *an apothecary*
MONSIEUR BONNEFOY, *a notary*
TOINETTE, *a maidservant*

ACT ONE

Scene 1

ARGAN: *(Alone in his room, adding up his apothecary's bills using tokens on a board. He speaks the following dialogue to himself.)* Three and two make five, and five make ten, and ten make twenty. Three and two make five. "Plus, on the twenty-fourth, a small insinuative, preparative, and emollient clyster, to mollify, humidify, and refresh Monsieur's inward parts..." What I like about Monsieur Fleurant, my apothecary, is that his bills are always so courteous: "...Monsieur's inward parts—thirty *sous*." Yes, Monsieur Fleurant, but being courteous isn't everything, you also have to be reasonable and not go fleecing sick people. Thirty sous for an enema: thank you very much, sir. You used to charge me twenty sous, and twenty sous in apothecary's language means ten sous—here's ten for you. "Plus, on the same day, a good detersive clyster, composed of double catholicon, rhubarb, rose-petal honey, and so on, according to the prescription, to sweep out, wash, and cleanse Monsieur's lower abdomen—thirty sous." With your permission—ten sous. "Plus, on the same day, in the evening, a hepatic julep, soporific and somniferous, composed to make Monsieur sleep—thirty-five sous." No complaints about that one, it really did put me to sleep. Ten, fifteen, sixteen—seventeen and a half. "Plus, on the twenty-fifth, a good purgative and corroborative

medicine, composed of fresh cassia with Levantine
senna, and so on, according to Monsieur Purgon's
prescription, to expel and evacuate Monsieur's bile—
four francs." Ah, Monsieur Fleurant, you're joking!
Sick people are still people. Monsieur Purgon didn't
tell you to charge four francs. Make it... make it three
francs—twenty... thirty sous. "Plus, on the same day,
a pain-killing and astringent potion to make Monsieur
rest—thirty sous." Right. That's ten... fifteen sous.
"Plus, on the twenty-sixth, a carminative clyster, to
drive out Monsieur's winds—thirty sous." Ten sous,
Monsieur Fleurant. "Plus Monsieur's clyster repeated
in the evening, as above—thirty sous." Monsieur
Fleurant, that's ten sous. "Plus, on the twenty-seventh,
a good compound medicine to hasten the departure
and drive out Monsieur's bad humors—three francs."
Right, that's twenty... thirty sous: I'm so pleased
you're being reasonable. "Plus, on the twenty-eighth,
a dose of whey, clarified and sweetened, to calm,
soothe, ease, and refresh Monsieur's blood—twenty
sous." Right—ten sous. "Plus, a cordial and preventive
potion, composed of a dozen grains of bezoar, lime
and grenadine syrups, and so on, as prescribed—five
francs." Ah, Monsieur Fleurant, easy now, please! If
you go on like this, nobody will want to be sick any
more. Make it four francs. That's twenty... forty sous.
Three and two make five, and five make ten, and ten
make twenty. Sixty-three francs, four and a half sous.
So, this month I've taken one, two, three, four, five,
six, seven, eight medicines; and one, two, three, four,
five, six, seven, eight, nine, ten, eleven, twelve enemas.
And last month it was twelve medicines and twenty
enemas. I'm not surprised that I don't feel as well this
month as I did the last. I'll tell Monsieur Purgon, so
that he can rectify it. Here, take all this away. (*He looks
around.*) There's nobody. Say what I like, they're never
here when I want them. (*He rings for his servants.*) They

don't hear, and my bell isn't loud enough. Jingle, jingle, jingle. Nothing happens. Jingle, jingle, jingle. They're deaf. Toinette! Jingle, jingle, jingle. Just as if I'm not ringing at all. Bitch! Slut! Jingle, jingle, jingle. It's infuriating! *(He stops ringing and shouts.)* Jingle, jingle, jingle! Pig! Damn it to hell! How can you leave a poor sick man all alone like this? Jingle, jingle, jingle! Oh, it's pitiful! Jingle, jingle, jingle! My God, they'll leave me here to die! Jingle, jingle, jingle!

Scene 2

TOINETTE: *(Enters)* We're off again!

ARGAN: Ah, you bitch! You slut!

TOINETTE: *(Pretending she has bumped her head)* Darn your impatience! You make us run around so much, I just bashed my head against the corner of the door.

ARGAN: *(Angrily)* Ah, you faker...!

TOINETTE: *(To interrupt him and keep him from shouting, goes on moaning)* Ohh!

ARGAN: It was...

TOINETTE: Ohh!

ARGAN: It was an hour ago...

TOINETTE: Ohh!

ARGAN: That you left me...

TOINETTE: Ohh!

ARGAN: Shut up, you slut, so I can yell at you.

TOINETTE: Oh, come on! That's all I need, after what I just did to myself.

ARGAN: You've made me hoarse, you pig.

TOINETTE: And you, you made me smash my head: the one's as good as the other, tit for tat, if you like.

ARGAN: What? You slut…

TOINETTE: If you yell, I'll cry.

ARGAN: Leave me, you faker…

TOINETTE: *(Still interrupting him)* Ohh!

ARGAN: Bitch, you want to…

TOINETTE: Ohh!

ARGAN: What? So again I won't have the pleasure of yelling at her?

TOINETTE: Go on, yell your head off.

ARGAN: You don't let me, bitch, you keep interrupting me.

TOINETTE: If you can have the pleasure of yelling, then I, for my part, should have the pleasure of crying: to each his own, it's only fair. Ohh!

ARGAN: All right, let's drop it. Clear this away, slut, clear it away. *(He gets up from his chair.)* My enema worked well today, didn't it?

TOINETTE: Your enema?

ARGAN: Yes, I produced a lot of bile, eh?

TOINETTE: My God, I don't meddle in things like that! Let Monsieur Fleurant poke his nose into it, since he profits from it.

ARGAN: See that they keep a bouillon ready for me, I have to take another one soon.

TOINETTE: That Monsieur Fleurant there and that Monsieur Purgon have lots of fun over your body; you're a good milk cow for them. I'd like to ask them what's wrong with you, since they give you so many treatments.

ARGAN: Quiet, ignorant woman, it's not for you to check the prescriptions of the medical profession. Send me my daughter Angélique, I have to tell her something.

TOINETTE: Here she comes herself. She's guessed your thoughts.

Scene 3

ARGAN: Come here, Angélique. You're just in time: I wanted to talk to you.

ANGÉLIQUE: Here I am, ready to listen.

ARGAN: *(Running off to the toilet)* Wait. Give me my stick. I'll be back in a minute.

TOINETTE: *(Mocking him)* Go quickly, Monsieur, go! Do your business! Monsieur Fleurant keeps us all busy.

Scene 4

ANGÉLIQUE: *(Looking at her with a languishing eye, says confidingly)* Toinette.

TOINETTE: What?

ANGÉLIQUE: Look at me a moment.

TOINETTE: Well, so I'm looking.

ANGÉLIQUE: Toinette.

TOINETTE: Well, so what—"Toinette"?

ANGÉLIQUE: Can't you guess what I want to talk about?

TOINETTE: I have a pretty good idea: about our young lover. Because all our conversations for the past six days have been about him; and you don't feel good if you're not talking about him every minute.

ANGÉLIQUE: Since you know that, why don't you start the conversation and spare me the trouble of dragging you into it?

TOINETTE: You never give me a chance, and you're so caught up in it, it's hard to know where to begin.

ANGÉLIQUE: I admit that I can never weary of talking to you about him, and my heart seizes every moment to open itself to you. But tell me, Toinette, do you disapprove of the feelings I have for him?

TOINETTE: I wouldn't dare.

ANGÉLIQUE: Am I wrong to abandon myself to these sweet sensations?

TOINETTE: I don't say so.

ANGÉLIQUE: And should I be insensible to the tender professions of the ardent passion he feels for me?

TOINETTE: God forbid!

ANGÉLIQUE: Tell me, now, don't you find, as I do, some touch of Heaven, some working of destiny, in the sudden chance of our acquaintance?

TOINETTE: Yes.

ANGÉLIQUE: Don't you find his coming to my defense without even knowing me the act of a perfect gentleman?

TOINETTE: Yes.

ANGÉLIQUE: That a man could not behave more generously?

TOINETTE: Right.

ANGÉLIQUE: And that he has done it all with the best grace in the world?

TOINETTE: Oh, yes!

ANGÉLIQUE: Don't you find, Toinette, that he's a very good-looking man?

TOINETTE: Certainly.

ANGÉLIQUE: That he has the nicest manner in the world?

TOINETTE: No doubt.

ANGÉLIQUE: That his speeches, like his acts, have something noble about them?

TOINETTE: That's for sure.

ANGÉLIQUE: That one could hear nothing more passionate than all that he has said to me?

TOINETTE: True.

ANGÉLIQUE: And that there's nothing more annoying than the constraint imposed on me, which stifles all exchange of the gentle urgings of this mutual ardor that Heaven inspires in us?

TOINETTE: You're right.

ANGÉLIQUE: But, my dear Toinette, do you think he loves me as much as he says?

TOINETTE: Aha! These things sometimes need a little backing up. The feigning of love looks a lot like truth; and I've seen great actors at it.

ANGÉLIQUE: Ah, Toinette, what are you saying! Alas, from the way he speaks, could it be possible that he's not telling me the truth?

TOINETTE: In any case, you'll soon be enlightened. And since he wrote to you yesterday that he had decided to ask for your hand in marriage, that will be a quick way to find out if he's telling you the truth or not. That will be the best proof.

ANGÉLIQUE: Ah, Toinette, if this man deceives me, I'll never believe another man as long as I live!

TOINETTE: Look, your father's coming back.

Scene 5

ARGAN: *(Sits in his chair)* Well, so, my daughter, I have news for you, which you may not be expecting: someone has asked for your hand in marriage. What? You laugh? Yes, it's amusing, this word "marriage"; young girls find nothing funnier. Ah, nature, nature! From what I can see, my daughter, I have no need to ask if you'd like to get married.

ANGÉLIQUE: I must do all that you're pleased to tell me to do, father.

ARGAN: I'm very glad to have such an obedient daughter. The matter's concluded, then, and I've promised you to him.

ANGÉLIQUE: It is for me, father, to blindly follow all your wishes.

ARGAN: My wife, your stepmother, wanted me to make a nun of you, and of your little sister Louison as well. She kept insisting on it.

TOINETTE: *(Softly)* The sweet thing has her reasons.

ARGAN: She didn't want to consent to this marriage, but I won out, and my word has been given.

ANGÉLIQUE: Ah, father, I'm so obliged to you for all your kindnesses!

TOINETTE: I'm truly grateful to you for this. It's the most sensible thing you've ever done in your life.

ARGAN: I have yet to see the young man, but I'm told I'll be pleased with him, and that you will be, too.

ANGÉLIQUE: I'm sure of it, father.

ARGAN: How so? Have you seen him?

ANGÉLIQUE: Since your consent authorizes me to open my heart to you, I will not hesitate to tell you that chance made us acquainted six days ago, and that the request made to you is a result of the inclination for each other which took hold of us at first sight.

ARGAN: They didn't tell me that; but I'm very glad, and so much the better if that's how things are. They say he's a big, good-looking boy.

ANGÉLIQUE: Yes, father.

ARGAN: Tall.

ANGÉLIQUE: That he is.

ARGAN: Personable.

ANGÉLIQUE: Most certainly.

ARGAN: Good-looking.

ANGÉLIQUE: Very good.

ARGAN: Sensible, good family.

ANGÉLIQUE: Quite.

ARGAN: Very respectable.

ANGÉLIQUE: The most respectable man in the world.

ARGAN: Speaks fluent Latin and Greek.

ANGÉLIQUE: That I didn't know.

ARGAN: And will qualify as a doctor in three days.

ANGÉLIQUE: Him, father?

ARGAN: Yes. Didn't he tell you that?

ANGÉLIQUE: No, actually. Who told you?

ARGAN: Monsieur Purgon.

ANGÉLIQUE: Does Monsieur Purgon know him?

ARGAN: What a question! He must know him, since he's his nephew.

ANGÉLIQUE: Cléante—Monsieur Purgon's nephew?

ARGAN: What Cléante? We're talking about the man who has asked for your hand in marriage.

ANGÉLIQUE: Why, yes!

ARGAN: Well, he's Monsieur Purgon's nephew, the son of his brother-in-law, Monsieur Diafoirus, the doctor. And this son is named Thomas Diafoirus, not Cléante. And we agreed to the marriage this morning—Monsieur Purgon, Monsieur Fleurant, and I—and tomorrow this future son-in-law is to be brought to me by his father. What is it? You're all flabbergasted?

ANGÉLIQUE: It's that I've just learned you were talking about one man, father, and I thought it was another.

TOINETTE: What, Monsieur? How could you have made this ridiculous plan? And with all your wealth, you'd marry your daughter to a doctor?

ARGAN: Yes. What are you butting in for, you impudent slut!

TOINETTE: My God, calm down! You immediately start swearing. Can't we talk things over without getting carried away? There, let's be coolheaded. Please tell me, what's your reason for such a marriage?

ARGAN: My reason is that, seeing myself sick and infirm as I am, I want to have myself a son-in-law and relations who are doctors, so that I can count on good help against my illness, have in my family the sources for the treatments necessary for me, and have quick access to consultations and prescriptions.

TOINETTE: Well, now, that's what you'd call a reason, and it's a pleasure to answer each other calmly. But, Monsieur, swear on your conscience: are you sick?

ARGAN: What do you mean, you slut? Am I sick? Am I sick? What impudence!

TOINETTE: Well, yes, Monsieur, you are sick, let's not quarrel about that! Yes, you're very sick, I agree, and more sick than you think: that's a fact. But your daughter must marry a husband for herself; and, since she's not sick at all, there's no need to give her a doctor.

ARGAN: It's for me that I'm giving her this doctor. And a kindhearted daughter ought to be delighted to marry whatever's useful for her father's health.

TOINETTE: Good lord! Monsieur, would you like me to give you a piece of friendly advice?

ARGAN: What is this advice?

TOINETTE: Don't even dream of this marriage.

ARGAN: And why not?

TOINETTE: Why not? Because your daughter will never consent to it.

ARGAN: She'll never consent to it?

TOINETTE: No.

ARGAN: My daughter?

TOINETTE: Your daughter. She'll tell you she has no use for Monsieur Diafoirus, nor for his son Thomas Diafoirus, nor for all the Diafoiruses in the world.

ARGAN: Well, I have use for them. And besides, the match is more advantageous than one might think. Monsieur Diafoirus has only this son for heir; and, what's more, Monsieur Purgon, who has no wife or children, is leaving him his entire fortune in support of this marriage; and Monsieur Purgon is a man who has a good eight thousand livres a year.

TOINETTE: He must have killed a lot of people, if he's made himself so rich.

ARGAN: Eight thousand a year is already something, without counting the father's fortune.

TOINETTE: Monsieur, that's all well and good; but I keep coming back to this: I advise you, just between us, to choose her another husband. She's not made to be Madame Diafoirus.

ARGAN: And, me, I want it that way.

TOINETTE: Pah, don't talk like that!

ARGAN: What do you mean, don't talk like that?

TOINETTE: Just don't!

ARGAN: And why shouldn't I?

TOINETTE: They'll say you don't know what you're talking about.

ARGAN: They can say what they like; but I say to you that I want her to do as I've promised.

TOINETTE: No, I'm sure she won't do it.

ARGAN: I'll make her do it.

TOINETTE: She won't do it, I tell you.

ARGAN: She'll do it, or I'll put her in a convent.

TOINETTE: You?

ARGAN: Me.

TOINETTE: Fine.

ARGAN: What do you mean, "fine"?

TOINETTE: You'll never put her in a convent.

ARGAN: I'll never put her in a convent?

TOINETTE: No.

ARGAN: No?

TOINETTE: No.

ARGAN: Oh, now, that's a good one: so I won't put my daughter in a convent if I want to?

TOINETTE: No, I'm telling you.

ARGAN: What's to stop me?

TOINETTE: You yourself.

ARGAN: Me?

TOINETTE: Yes, you won't have the heart.

ARGAN: I will too.

TOINETTE: You're fooling yourself.

ARGAN: I'm not fooling myself.

TOINETTE: Fatherly feelings will get the better of you.

ARGAN: No they won't.

TOINETTE: A little tear or two, arms thrown around your neck, a "my dear little papa," spoken tenderly, will be enough to touch you.

ARGAN: None of that will do anything.

TOINETTE: Yes, yes.

ARGAN: I tell you I'll never give in.

TOINETTE: Fiddlesticks.

ARGAN: Don't ever say "fiddlesticks".

TOINETTE: My God! I know you, you're naturally good.

ARGAN: *(Angrily)* I'm not good at all, and I can be bad when I want to be.

TOINETTE: Calmly, Monsieur: you're forgetting that you're sick.

ARGAN: I absolutely order her to prepare herself to take whatever husband I tell her to.

TOINETTE: And I absolutely forbid her to do anything of the sort.

ARGAN: Where is this getting us? And what is this audacity in a slut of a maidservant, to speak like that to her master?

TOINETTE: When a master doesn't know what he's doing, a sensible maidservant is right to correct him.

ARGAN: *(Runs after her)* Ah, you insolent…! I'll knock you down!

TOINETTE: *(Runs away from him)* It is my duty to oppose things that could dishonor you.

ARGAN: *(Angry, chases her around his chair, stick in hand)* Come here, come here, I'll teach you how to talk.

TOINETTE: *(Running, and hiding herself behind the opposite side of the chair from* ARGAN*)* I am interested, as I should be, in not letting you do anything foolish.

ARGAN: Bitch!

TOINETTE: No, I shall never consent to this marriage.

ARGAN: Scum!

TOINETTE: I never want her to marry your Thomas Diafoirus.

ARGAN: Pig!

TOINETTE: And she'll obey me and not you.

ARGAN: Angélique, why don't you catch this slut for me?

ANGÉLIQUE: Oh, father, you mustn't make yourself sick.

ARGAN: If you don't catch her for me, I'll put my curse on you.

TOINETTE: And I'll disinherit her if she obeys you.

ARGAN: *(Throws himself into his chair, worn out from running after her)* Ah! Ah! I can't go on. It'll be the death of me.

Scene 6

ARGAN: Ah, my wife! Come here.

BÉLINE: What's wrong, my poor husband?

ARGAN: Come and help me.

BÉLINE: What on earth is it, my little one?

ARGAN: My pet.

BÉLINE: My love.

ARGAN: They just made me angry.

BÉLINE: Alas, poor little husband. How so, my love?

ARGAN: Your slut of a Toinette has grown more insolent than ever.

BÉLINE: You mustn't get so worked up.

ARGAN: She made me furious, my pet.

BÉLINE: Calm yourself, my little one.

ARGAN: For a whole hour now, she's kept me from doing what I want.

BÉLINE: There, there, keep calm.

ARGAN: And she had the nerve to tell me I'm not even sick.

BÉLINE: She's an impertinent thing.

ARGAN: Dear heart, you know what's what.

BÉLINE: Yes, dear heart, she's wrong.

ARGAN: This slut will be the death of me, love.

BÉLINE: There, there, now.

ARGAN: She's the cause of all the bile I produce.

BÉLINE: Don't get so upset.

ARGAN: And I don't know how many times I've told you to rid me of her.

BÉLINE: My God, little one, there are no servants without their faults. One is sometimes forced to suffer their bad qualities for the sake of the good. This one is skilful, meticulous, diligent, and above all faithful, and you know that nowadays one has to take great precautions with the people one hires. Hey there! Toinette!

TOINETTE: Madame.

BÉLINE: Why have you made my husband angry?

TOINETTE: *(In a sugary tone)* I, Madame? Alas, I don't know what you're trying to say. I think only of pleasing Monsieur in everything.

ARGAN: Ah, the faker!

TOINETTE: He told us he wanted to give his daughter in marriage to the son of Monsieur Diafoirus. I replied to him that I found the match advantageous for her, but that it would be better if he put her in a convent.

BÉLINE: There's no great harm in that. I even think she's right.

ARGAN: Ah, love, you believe her? She's a villain: she said a hundred insolent things to me.

BÉLINE: All right, I believe you, my love! Now, pull yourself together. Listen, Toinette, if you ever annoy my husband, I'll throw you out. Here, give me his fur-lined cloak and some pillows, so that I can make him comfortable in his chair. Just look at you! Pull your nightcap down over your ears: there's nothing that causes a cold like air blowing in your ears.

ARGAN: Ah, my pet, I'm so obliged to you for all the care you take of me!

BÉLINE: *(Adjusting the pillows around Argan)* Raise yourself so I can put this under you. Let's put this one so you can lean on it, and this one on the other side.

Let's put this one behind your back, and this other one to support your head.

TOINETTE: (*Rudely jamming a pillow on his head and running off*) And this one to keep you from the evening dew.

ARGAN: (*Rises up in anger and throws all the pillows at Toinette*) Ah, you slut, you want to smother me!

BÉLINE: There, there! What is all this?

ARGAN: (*Out of breath, throws himself into his chair*) Oh, oh, oh! I can't go on!

BÉLINE: Why do you get so carried away? She meant to be helpful.

ARGAN: You have no idea, love, how malicious the slut is. Ah, I'm completely beside myself! It'll take eight medicines and a dozen enemas to remedy it all.

BÉLINE: There, there, my little one, just calm down.

ARGAN: My pet, you're my only consolation.

BÉLINE: Poor little one.

ARGAN: To try and repay you for the love you bear me, as I've told you, dear heart, I wish to make my will.

BÉLINE: Ah, my love, let us not speak of that, I beg you: I cannot bear the thought of it. The word "will" alone makes me shake with grief.

ARGAN: I told you to speak to your notary about it.

BÉLINE: He's just outside. I brought him with me.

ARGAN: Have him come in, then, my pet.

BÉLINE: Alas, my love, when you really love your husband, you're hardly able to think of all that.

Scene 7

ARGAN: Come here, Monsieur de Bonnefoy, come here.
Sit down, please. My wife has told me, Monsieur, that
you are a very honest man and one of her good friends;
and I have asked her to speak to you about a will I
wish to make.

BÉLINE: Alas, I cannot speak of these things.

NOTARY: She has explained your intentions to me,
Monsieur, and the plan you have in mind for her,
regarding which, I must tell you, you will not be able
to leave your wife anything in your will.

ARGAN: But why?

NOTARY: Common Law is against it. If you lived in a
land of statutory law, it could be done; but in Paris,
and in common law lands, or at least in most of them,
it cannot be done, and the disposition would be null
and void. The only way a man and woman joined by
matrimony can benefit each other is by donation *inter
vivos*; and then only if there are no children, either of
the two together, or of one of them, at the time of death
of the first to die.

ARGAN: It's a rather impertinent Common Law, that
says a husband can't leave anything to a wife who
loves him tenderly and takes such good care of him. I'd
like to consult my lawyer, to see what I may be able to
do.

NOTARY: It's not lawyers you should turn to, because
as a rule they're usually rather strict about such
things, and think it a great crime to go around the law.
They're pedants, and know nothing of the intricacies
of conscience. There are other people to consult, who
are much more accommodating, who have ways of
quietly passing over the law, of justifying what's
not permitted; who know how to smooth out the

difficulties of an affair, and find means of eluding the Common Law by some indirect route. Without that, how would we get along day by day? You have to have a knack for things; otherwise we'd get nothing done, and our profession wouldn't be worth a cent.

ARGAN: My wife rightly said, Monsieur, that you were a very skillful man, and a very honest one. Kindly tell me, how shall I go about leaving her my fortune and depriving my children of it?

NOTARY: How to go about it? You can carefully choose a close friend of your wife's, to whom you will give as much as you can in due form by means of your will; and this friend will then hand it all over to her. You can also acquire a large number of bonds, quite legitimate ones, to the profit of various creditors, who will then sign them over to your wife, and declare that they have done so as a gift to her. While you live, you can also hand over ready cash to her, or notes payable to the bearer.

BÉLINE: My God, you mustn't torment yourself with all this! If it comes to being without you, my little one, I do not wish to remain in this world.

ARGAN: My pet!

BÉLINE: Yes, my love, if I am so unfortunate as to lose you...

ARGAN: My dear wife!

BÉLINE: Life will be nothing to me any more.

ARGAN: Love!

BÉLINE: And I shall follow in your footsteps, so that you know the tenderness I have for you.

ARGAN: My pet, you're breaking my heart. Console yourself, I beg you.

NOTARY: These tears are out of season. Things haven't come to that yet.

BÉLINE: Ah, Monsieur, you don't know what it is to have a husband one loves tenderly.

ARGAN: My only regret, if I die, my pet, is to have no child by you. Monsieur Purgon told me he'd get me to make one.

NOTARY: It might still come.

ARGAN: I must make my will, love, the way Monsieur says. But, as a precaution, I want to hand you over twenty thousand francs in gold, which I keep behind the paneling in my bedroom, and two notes payable to the bearer, which are owed to me—one by Monsieur Damon, and the other by Monsieur Gérante.

BÉLINE: No, no, I don't want all that. Ah! How much did you say there is in your bedroom?

ARGAN: Twenty thousand francs, love.

BÉLINE: Don't talk to me about money, I beg you. Ah! How much are the two notes worth?

ARGAN: One is for four thousand francs, my pet, and the other is for six.

BÉLINE: All the riches in the world, my love, aren't worth the price of you.

NOTARY: Shall we proceed with the will?

ARGAN: Yes, Monsieur, but we'd better go to my little study. Lead me there, love, please.

BÉLINE: Come, my poor little one.

Scene 8

TOINETTE: So they're with the notary, and I heard talk of a will. Your stepmother's no sluggard. She's undoubtedly pushing your father into some conspiracy against your interests.

ANGÉLIQUE: He can dispose of his fortune as he likes, so long as he doesn't dispose of my heart. You see, Toinette, what violent designs they have on it. Please don't abandon me in the plight I'm in.

TOINETTE: Me, abandon you? I'd rather die. Let your stepmother make me her confidante and try to draw me to her side. I've never had any liking for her, and I've always been on your side. Let me handle it: I'll use every means to serve you; but to serve you more effectively, I'm going to change my tactics, hide what I feel for you, and pretend to side with your father and your stepmother.

ANGÉLIQUE: Try, I beg you, to get word to Cléante about the marriage they've arranged.

TOINETTE: I've got nobody to give that errand to except the old usurer Punchinello, my lover, and it will cost me a few sweet nothings, which I'll gladly spend for you. It's too late today; but tomorrow, first thing, I'll send for him, and he'll be delighted to...

BÉLINE: Toinette!

TOINETTE: They're calling me. Good night. Count on me.

(Curtain)

END OF ACT ONE

ACT TWO

Scene 1

(Same room as in ACT ONE)

TOINETTE: What do you want, Monsieur?

CLÉANTE: What do I want?

TOINETTE: Ah, it's you? What a surprise! What have you come here for?

CLÉANTE: To learn my fate, to speak to kind Angélique, consult the feelings of her heart, and ask her decision on this fatal marriage I have been informed of.

TOINETTE: Yes, but one doesn't speak straight out like that to Angélique: one needs to be mysterious. And you've been told how strictly she's watched over, that she's not allowed to go out or to speak to anyone, and that it was only through the curiosity of an old aunt that we were granted permission to go to that play which saw the birth of your passion; and we've avoided all talk about that adventure.

CLÉANTE: That's why I haven't come here as Cléante, her suitor, but as a friend of her music teacher, who has allowed me to say that he's sending me in his place.

TOINETTE: Here's her father. Back off a little, and let me tell him you're here.

Scene 2

ARGAN: Monsieur Purgon told me to walk in my room in the morning, twelve times up and twelve times down; but I forgot to ask him if was lengthwise or widthwise.

TOINETTE: Monsieur, here is a...

ARGAN: Talk softly, slut: you've just scrambled my whole brain. Don't you realize that you mustn't talk so loud to sick people?

TOINETTE: I wanted to tell you, Monsieur...

ARGAN: Talk softly, I tell you.

TOINETTE: Monsieur... *(She pretends to say something.)*

ARGAN: Eh?

TOINETTE: I tell you that... *(She pretends to say something.)*

ARGAN: What did you say?

TOINETTE: *(Loudly)* I say there's a man here who wants to speak to you.

ARGAN: Show him in.

Toinette makes a sign for Cléante to step forward.

CLÉANTE: Monsieur...

TOINETTE: *(Mockingly)* Don't talk so loud, or you risk scrambling Monsieur's brain.

CLÉANTE: Monsieur, I'm delighted to find you up and about, and to see that you're feeling better.

TOINETTE: *(Pretending to be angry)* What do you mean, "feeling better." That's not so: Monsieur always feels bad.

CLÉANTE: I heard that Monsieur was better, and I find he looks well.

TOINETTE: What do you mean by your "looks well"? Monsieur looks awful, and they were impertinent fools who told you he was better. He's never felt worse.

ARGAN: She's right.

TOINETTE: He walks, sleeps, eats and drinks like everybody else; but that doesn't mean he's not terribly sick.

ARGAN: It's true.

CLÉANTE: Monsieur, I'm desperately sorry. I've come at the request of your daughter's singing teacher. He has been obliged to go to the country for a few days; and as his close friend, he has sent me in his place, to continue her lessons, lest by interrupting them she should come to forget what she already knows.

ARGAN: Very good. (*To* TOINETTE) Call Angélique.

TOINETTE: I believe, Monsieur, that it will be better to take Monsieur to her room.

ARGAN: No, have her come.

TOINETTE: He cannot give her a proper lesson if they're not alone.

ARGAN: Yes he can, he can.

TOINETTE: Monsieur, you'll find it noisy, and nothing must upset you in the state you're in and scramble your brain.

ARGAN: Not at all, not at all: I love music, and I'll be very happy to… Ah, here she is! You, go and see if my wife is dressed.

Scene 3

ARGAN: Come here, my daughter. Your music teacher has gone to the country, and here is a person he has sent in his place to instruct you.

ANGÉLIQUE: Oh, heavens!

ARGAN: What is it? Why are you so surprised?

ANGÉLIQUE: It's…

ARGAN: What? Why does he upset you so?

ANGÉLIQUE: It's just such a surprising coincidence, father.

ARGAN: How so?

ANGÉLIQUE: I dreamed last night that I was in the greatest predicament in the world, and that a person looking exactly like Monsieur appeared to me. I had asked him for help, and he had come to deliver me from the trouble I was in. I was greatly surprised, on coming here, to see the same man I had had in my mind all night.

CLÉANTE: I find it no misfortune to occupy your thoughts, whether asleep or awake, and my happiness would undoubtedly be great if you were in some sort of trouble from which you judged me worthy to deliver you. There's nothing I would not do for…

Scene 4

TOINETTE: (To ARGAN, derisively) Well, Monsieur, I'm on your side now, and I take back all that I said yesterday. Monsieur Diafoirus the father and Monsieur Diafoirus the son have come to pay you a visit. You're going to be well son-in-lawed! You're about to see the best-looking boy in the world, and the wittiest. He said only a couple of words, but they delighted me, and your daughter will be charmed by him.

ARGAN: *(To* CLÉANTE, *who makes as if to leave)* Don't leave, Monsieur. I'm marrying off my daughter, and they're bringing the husband-to-be, whom she hasn't seen yet.

CLÉANTE: You honor me greatly, Monsieur, in wanting me to witness so pleasant a meeting.

ARGAN: He's the son of an able doctor, and the marriage will take place in four days.

CLÉANTE: Very good.

ARGAN: Send word to her music teacher, so that he can attend the wedding.

CLÉANTE: I shall do so without fail.

ARGAN: You come, too.

CLÉANTE: You do me great honor.

TOINETTE: Come, take your places, they're here.

Scene 5

ARGAN: *(Raising his hand to his nightcap without taking it off)* Monsieur Purgon has forbidden me to uncover my head, Monsieur. You're of the same profession, you know the consequences.

DIAFOIRUS: All our visits are intended to bring help to the sick, not to inconvenience them.

*(*ARGAN *and* DIAFOIRUS *speak at the same time, interrupting and confusing each other.)*

ARGAN: I receive, Monsieur…

DIAFOIRUS: We have come, Monsieur…

ARGAN: …with great joy…

DIAFOIRUS: ...my son Thomas and I...

ARGAN: ...the honor you do me...

DIAFOIRUS: ...to show you, Monsieur...

ARGAN: ...and would have wished...

DIAFOIRUS: ...how delighted we are...

ARGAN: ...I were able to call on you...

DIAFOIRUS: ...with the favor you have shown us...

ARGAN: ...to assure you of it...

DIAFOIRUS: ...in so kindly receiving us...

ARGAN: ...but you know, Monsieur...

DIAFOIRUS: ...into the honor, Monsieur...

ARGAN: ...how it is for a poor sick man...

DIAFOIRUS: ...of your alliance...

ARGAN: ...who can do nothing else...

DIAFOIRUS: ...and assure you...

ARGAN: ...than say to you here...

DIAFOIRUS: ...that in things dependant upon our profession...

ARGAN: ...that he shall seek every occasion...

DIAFOIRUS: ...as in all others...

ARGAN: ...to make it known to you, Monsieur...

DIAFOIRUS: ...we shall always be ready...

ARGAN: ...that he is entirely at your service.

DIAFOIRUS: ...to show you our zeal. *(He turns to his son and says to him)* Come, Thomas, step forward. Pay your compliments.

THOMAS: I should begin with the father, shouldn't I?

DIAFOIRUS: Yes.

THOMAS: Monsieur, I come to greet, acknowledge, cherish, and revere in you a second father; but a second father to whom I dare say I find myself more indebted than to the first. The first engendered me, but you have chosen me. He received me by necessity, but you have accepted me by grace. What I have from him is a work of his body, but what I have from you is a work of your will. And the more that the spiritual faculties are above the corporeal, so much the more do I owe you, and so much the more do I hold precious this future filiation, of which I come today to render you in advance my most humble and most respectful gratitude.

TOINETTE: Long live the schools that can produce such a gifted man!

THOMAS: Did I do well, father?

DIAFOIRUS: *Optime.*

ARGAN: *(To* ANGÉLIQUE*)* Come, greet the gentleman.

THOMAS: Do I kiss her?

DIAFOIRUS: Yes, yes.

THOMAS: *(To* ANGÉLIQUE*)* Madame, it is with full justice that Heaven has bestowed upon you the name of stepmother, for in your every step…

ARGAN: She's not my wife, she's my daughter.

THOMAS: Where is your wife, then?

ARGAN: She's coming.

THOMAS: Do I wait till she comes, father?

DIAFOIRUS: You can still pay your compliments to Mademoiselle.

THOMAS: Mademoiselle, just as the statue of Memnon gave forth a harmonious sound the moment it was lit by the rays of the sun, so do I feel animated by a sweet transport at the appearance of the sunlight of your beauty. And as naturalists observe that the flower known as heliotrope turns incessantly towards this star of day, so my heart henceforward will ever turn towards the shining stars of your adorable eyes, as towards its only pole. Today, then, Mademoiselle, allow me to lay upon the altar of your charms the offering of this heart, which neither respires nor seeks any other glory than to be all its life, Mademoiselle, your most humble, most obedient, and most faithful servant and husband.

TOINETTE: *(Mocking him)* That's what studying can do: you learn to say such fine things!

ARGAN: *(To* CLÉANTE*)* Well, what do you say to that?

CLÉANTE: That Monsieur does wonders, and if he's as good a doctor as he is an orator, it will be a pleasure to be one of his patients.

TOINETTE: Definitely. It will be an admirable thing if his cures turn out as fine as his speeches.

ARGAN: Come, quickly, my chair, and seats for everybody. Put yourself here, my daughter. You see, Monsieur, that everyone admires Monsieur your son, and I find you quite fortunate, seeing you have such a son.

DIAFOIRUS: Monsieur, it is not because I am his father, but I may say that I have reason to be pleased with him, and that all who see him speak of him as a boy who has no wickedness in him. He has never had the lively imagination nor the sparkling wit that is to be found in some; but it is that which has always made me foresee the best for his good judgment, a quality called for in the exercise of our art. When he was little, he was never what's known as sharp and alert. One always found him gentle, peaceful, and taciturn, never saying a word, and never playing at all those little things known as children's games. We had all

the trouble in the world teaching him to read, and at
the age of nine he still hadn't learned the alphabet.
"Good," I said to myself, "it's the late trees that bear
the best fruit; it's much harder to carve in marble
than in sand, but things last much longer in it, and
this slowness of comprehension, this sluggishness of
imagination, is the mark of good judgment to come."
When I sent him away to school, he had a hard time
of it; but he braced himself against the difficulties,
and his masters always praised him to me for his
assiduousness and effort. At last, by hammering away,
he arrived gloriously at attaining his diplomas; and
I may say without vanity that for the two years that
he has been a doctoral candidate, there is no student
who has made more noise than he in all of our school's
debates. He has made himself formidable, and no act
is passed in which he has not argued all out for the
contrary proposition. He is firm in dispute, strong
as a Turk on his principles, never budges an inch in
his opinions, and pursues his argument to the last
recesses of logic. But what pleases me above all in
him, and here he follows my example, is that he is
blindly attached to the opinions of our elders, and has
never wished to understand or even hear about the
arguments and experiments of the so-called discoveries
of our age concerning the circulation of the blood and
other opinions of the same ilk.

THOMAS: (*Pulls a large rolled up thesis from his pocket
and presents it to* ANGÉLIQUE) I have defended a thesis
against these circulators, which, with Monsieur's
permission, I venture to present to Mademoiselle, as an
homage I owe her of the first fruits of my mind.

ANGÉLIQUE: Monsieur, for me it's a useless piece of
furniture. I know nothing about such things.

TOINETTE: Give it, give it, it's worth taking just for the
cover. It will make a nice decoration for our room.

THOMAS: Again with Monsieur's permission, I invite
you to come one of these days and amuse yourself by
watching the dissection of a woman, upon which I am
to give a commentary.

TOINETTE: That will be a pleasant amusement. There
are some who treat their mistresses to a play; but
treating them to a dissection is something much more
gallant.

DIAFOIRUS: Moreover, as regards the qualities required
for marriage and propagation, I assure you that,
according to the rules of our fellow doctors, he is all
that can be desired, that he possesses the prolific virtue
to an admirable degree, and is of the temperament
needed for engendering and procreating well-made
children.

ARGAN: Is it not your intention, Monsieur, to push him
at Court and get him a position as doctor there?

DIAFOIRUS: Frankly speaking, our professional relations
with the great have never seemed very agreeable
to me, and I have always found it more worthwhile
for us to keep to the general public. The public is
accommodating. You don't have to answer to anyone
for your actions; and provided you follow the current
rules of the art, you're not to blame for whatever may
result. What's annoying with the great is that, when
they happen to get sick, they really want their doctors
to cure them.

TOINETTE: That's funny. And how impertinent of them
to want you Monsieurs to cure them: you're not there
for that; you're only there to collect your fees and
prescribe them treatments; it's up to them to get cured
if they can.

DIAFOIRUS: That's true. We're only obliged to treat
people in the customary way.

ARGAN: *(To* CLÉANTE*)* Monsieur, have my daughter
sing a little something for the company.

CLÉANTE: I was waiting for your orders, Monsieur.
And to amuse the company it has occurred to me to
sing a scene with Mademoiselle from a little opera that
was performed recently. Here, this is your part.

ANGÉLIQUE: Me?

CLÉANTE: *(Softly, to* ANGÉLIQUE*)* Please don't refuse.
(Aloud) Let me explain to you what scene we will
sing. I have no singing voice; but it's enough if I make
myself heard. I hope I may be excused by the need to
have Mademoiselle sing.

ARGAN: Is it good verse?

CLÉANTE: It's just a little impromptu opera. All you'll
hear sung is rhythmic prose, or a sort of free verse,
such as passion and necessity can make two persons
speak, when talking spontaneously and off the cuff.

ARGAN: Very well. Let's listen.

(In the person of a shepherd, CLÉANTE *explains to his
mistress his love since their first meeting; then they express
their thoughts to each other in song.)*

CLÉANTE: Here is the subject of the scene. A Shepherd
was appreciating the beauties of a play that had just
begun, when his attention was drawn to a noise he
heard beside him. He turns and sees a brute who
is abusing a Shepherdess with insolent words. He
at once takes the side of the sex to which all men
owe homage; and after punishing the brute for his
insolence, he goes up to the Shepherdess, and sees a
young girl who, from the most beautiful eyes he has
ever seen, is pouring out tears which he finds the most
beautiful in the world. "Alas," he says to himself, "is
anyone capable of offending so lovable a person? And
how inhuman, how barbaric not to be moved by such

tears." He takes care to dry those tears that he finds so
beautiful; and the lovable Shepherdess takes care at the
same time to thank him for his slight service, but in so
charming, so tender, and so passionate a way that the
Shepherd cannot resist it; and each word, each glance,
is a fiery dart by which his heart feels pierced. "Is there
anything," he says, "that can deserve the loving words
of such thanks? And what would one not do, to what
services, to what dangers would one not be delighted
to run, to attract a single moment of the touching
sweetness of so thankful a soul?" The whole play goes
by without his paying any attention; but he complains
that it is too short, because in ending it will separate
him from his adorable Shepherdess. And from this first
glimpse, from this first moment, he takes home with
him a love as passionate as one that has lasted several
years. At once he feels all the pangs of absence, and he
is tormented to see no more what he saw so briefly. He
does all he can to catch again that glimpse, of which,
day and night, he keeps so dear a notion; but the great
constraint in which his Shepherdess is kept leaves
him no means. The violence of his passion makes him
resolve to ask for the hand of the sweet beauty without
whom he can no longer live, and he obtains her
permission by means of a letter which he manages to
send her. But at the same time he is informed that the
beauty's father has arranged her marriage to another,
and that the ceremony is about to take place. Judge
what a cruel blow it is to the sad Shepherd's heart.
Behold him overcome with mortal sorrow. He cannot
bear the frightful idea of seeing all that he loves in the
arms of another; and his desperate love makes him
find a way of insinuating himself into the house of his
Shepherdess, in order to learn her feelings and know
from her the destiny he must resign himself to. There
he finds the preparations for all that he fears; he sees
the coming of the unworthy rival, whom a father's

caprice has set against the tender feelings of his love.
He sees him, this ridiculous rival, triumphant beside
the lovable Shepherdess, as beside a conquest assured
to him; and this sight fills him with an anger he is
barely able to master. He casts sorrowful glances at the
one he adores; but his respect, and the presence of her
father, keep him from saying anything except with his
eyes. Finally, however, he breaks all constraint, and
the transport of his love obliges him to speak thus. *(He
sings:)*

> Lovely Phyllis, the suffering is too great;
> Break this hard silence, open your thoughts to me.
> Teach me my destiny.
> Life, or death—which is to be my fate?

ANGÉLIQUE: *(Replies, singing)*
> You see me, Tircis, sad and melancholy,
> Preparing for the hymen you fear so.
> I raise my eyes to heaven, I look at you, I sigh,
> There is no more to know.

ARGAN: Well, now! I had no idea my daughter was
clever enough to sight-read like that without any
hesitation.

CLÉANTE:
> Alas! Lovely Phyllis,
> Can it be your amorous Tircis
> Should have so fair a part
> As to find himself a place in your dear heart?

ANGÉLIQUE:
> Oh, now I fear no judgment from above:
> Yes, Tircis, thee I love.

CLÉANTE:
> O most charming word!
> But have I rightly heard?
> Say it again! I hope I have not erred.

ANGÉLIQUE:
> Yes, Tircis, thee I love.

CLÉANTE:
> Once more, Phyllis, I pray.

ANGÉLIQUE:
> I love thee.

CLÉANTE:
> Repeat it a hundred times, oh, never weary!

ANGÉLIQUE:
> I love thee, I love thee,
>> Yes, Tircis, thee I love.

CLÉANTE:
> Gods, kings, who see the whole world at your feet,
> Can you compare your happiness to mine?
>> And yet, Phyllis, one thought
>> Comes to trouble this sweet transport:
>>> A rival, a rival…

ANGÉLIQUE:
> Ah, I hate him worse than death!
> For me his presence, as for you,
>> Is a cruel torment.

CLÉANTE:
> But a father would subject you to his wishes.

ANGÉLIQUE:
>> Sooner, sooner die
>> Than ever give him my consent;
> Sooner, sooner die, oh, sooner die.

ARGAN: And what does the father say to all that?

CLÉANTE: Nothing.

ARGAN: There's a foolish father for you, to suffer all this foolishness without saying anything.

CLÉANTE:
>> Ah! my love…

ARGAN: No, no, enough. That play sets a very bad example. The shepherd Tircis is impertinent, and the shepherdess Phyllis is impudent, to talk like that in front of her father. Show me that paper. Ah! Where are the words you spoke? There's nothing here but music.

CLÉANTE: Don't you know, Monsieur, that they recently invented a way of writing words with the notes themselves?

ARGAN: Fine. Thank you very much, Monsieur, and good-bye. We could have done without your impertinent opera.

CLÉANTE: I hoped to amuse you.

ARGAN: Foolishness is not amusing. Ah, here's my wife!

Scene 6

ARGAN: Love, here's Monsieur Diafoirus's son.

THOMAS: *(Begins a compliment he has studied, but memory fails him and he cannot go on)* Madame, it is with full justice that Heaven has bestowed upon you the name of stepmother, for in your every step…

BÉLINE: Monsieur, I am delighted to have come here so opportunely as to have the honor of seeing you.

THOMAS: For in your every step… for in your every step… Madame, you interrupted me in the middle of a phrase, and I forgot what I was saying.

DIAFOIRUS: Keep it for another time, Thomas.

ARGAN: I wish, my pet, you had been here just now.

TOINETTE: Ah, Madame, you've really lost out, not being here for the second father, the statue of Memnon, and the flower called heliotrope.

ARGAN: Come, my daughter, take Monsieur's hand, and give him your word, as you would to your husband.

ANGÉLIQUE: Father...

ARGAN: "Father"? What's that supposed to mean?

ANGÉLIQUE: I beg you, don't rush things. At least give us time to get to know each other, and to see born in us that inclination for each other so necessary in forming a perfect union.

THOMAS: For my part, Mademoiselle, it is already fully born in me, and I have no need to wait any longer.

ANGÉLIQUE: If you are so quick, Monsieur, it is not the same for me, and I confess to you that your merit has not yet made a sufficient impression on my soul.

ARGAN: Oh, all right, all right! There'll be time enough for that, once you two are married.

ANGÉLIQUE: Ah, father, give me time, I pray you. Marriage is a chain that a heart must never be forced to submit to. And if Monsieur is an honest man, he will never want to accept a person who is made his by force.

THOMAS: *Nego consequentiam*, Mademoiselle. I can be an honest man and still want to accept you from Monsieur your father's hands.

ANGÉLIQUE: To do violence to someone is a wicked way of making oneself loved.

THOMAS: We read in the ancients, Mademoiselle, that their custom with the girls they wanted to marry was to carry them off by force from their father's house, so it would appear that it was not by their consent that they were conjoined with a man.

ANGÉLIQUE: The ancients, Monsieur, were the ancients, and we are people of today. Pretences are not necessary in our time; and when a marriage pleases us, we know very well how to enter into it without being dragged. Grant me patience. If you love me, Monsieur, you should want all that I want.

THOMAS: Yes, Mademoiselle, but only so far as my love is concerned.

ANGÉLIQUE: But the great sign of love is to submit to the wishes of the woman you love.

THOMAS: *Distinguo*, Mademoiselle. In what does not concern his property, *concedo*; but in what does concern it, *nego*.

TOINETTE: You're wasting your time arguing: Monsieur is fresh from school, he will always one-up you. Why resist so much, and refuse the glory of being attached to a member of the Faculty?

BÉLINE: Perhaps she has some other inclination in her head.

ANGÉLIQUE: If I did, Madame, it would be such as reason and decency could allow.

ARGAN: Well, I'm playing a funny role here!

BÉLINE: If I were you, my dear, I wouldn't force her to marry. And I know very well what I *would* do.

ANGÉLIQUE: I know what you wish to say, Madame, and all the kindness you have for me; but perhaps your advice will not have the good fortune to be followed.

BÉLINE: Such wise and decent girls as you don't care about being obedient and submissive to the will of their fathers. Things used to be better.

ANGÉLIQUE: The duty of a daughter has limits, Madame, and neither reason nor law extends it to all sorts of things.

BÉLINE: Which is to say that your thoughts are not against marriage, but you want to choose a husband of your own fancy.

ANGÉLIQUE: If my father does not want to give me a husband who pleases me, I would beseech him at least not to force me to marry one whom I cannot love.

ARGAN: Messieurs, I beg your pardon for all this.

ANGÉLIQUE: Each of us has his own aim in marrying. As for me, who want only a husband I can truly love, and who intend to remain attached to him all my life, let me tell you that I will choose carefully. There are some who take husbands only so as to escape the constraints of their parents and be in a position to do whatever they like. There are others, Madame, who make marriage a business of pure self-interest, who marry only to gain a settlement, to enrich themselves by the death of those they marry, and run without scruple through one husband after another, so as to appropriate their spoils. Such women, truly, do not stand much on ceremony and pay little attention to the man himself.

BÉLINE: I find you full of arguments today, and would like very much to know what you mean to say.

ANGÉLIQUE: I, Madame? What could I mean to say but what I have said?

BÉLINE: You're such a fool, my pet, you've become quite insufferable.

ANGÉLIQUE: You would like to make me answer you with some impertinence, Madame, but I warn you that you will not have that advantage.

BÉLINE: Nothing can match your insolence.

ANGÉLIQUE: No, Madame, you're wasting your breath.

BÉLINE: And you have a ridiculous pride, an impertinent presumption that makes the whole world shrug you off.

ANGÉLIQUE: This is all to no avail, Madame. I shall be sensible in spite of you; and to remove any hope that you may succeed in what you wish, I shall remove myself from your sight.

ARGAN: *(To* ANGÉLIQUE *as she leaves)* Listen, there's no middle way here: in four days you must choose to marry either Monsieur, or a convent. *(To* BÉLINE*)* Don't bother with it, I'll handle her.

BÉLINE: I'm sorry to leave you, little one, but I have some business in town which I cannot put off. I'll be back soon.

ARGAN: Go, love, and pass by your notary, have him speed up the you-know-what.

BÉLINE: Good-bye, my little friend.

ARGAN: Good-bye, my pet. There's a woman who loves me…it's unbelievable.

DIAFOIRUS: We shall take our leave of you, Monsieur.

ARGAN: Please, Monsieur, tell how I am.

DIAFOIRUS: *(Takes his pulse)* Come, Thomas, take Monsieur by the other arm, to see if you're able to read his pulse correctly. *Quid dicis?*

THOMAS: *Dico* that Monsieur's pulse is the pulse of a man who is not in good health.

DIAFOIRUS: Good.

THOMAS: That it is hardish, not to say hard.

DIAFOIRUS: Very good.

THOMAS: Pitapatatious.

DIAFOIRUS: *Bene.*

THOMAS: And even a bit capritatious.

DIAFOIRUS: *Optime.*

THOMAS: Which is the sign of an intemperance in the *splenetic parenchyma*—that is, the spleen.

DIAFOIRUS: Very good.

ARGAN: No. Monsieur Purgon says it's my liver that's sick.

DIAFOIRUS: Why, yes! To say *parenchyma* is to say the one and the other, because of the strict sympathy between them, by means of the *vas breve* of the *pylorus*, and often of the *meatus choledici*. No doubt he prescribes that you eat a lot of roast beef.

ARGAN: No, only boiled.

DIAFOIRUS: Ah, yes! Well, roasted or boiled, it's all the same. His prescription is very prudent, and you couldn't be in better hands.

ARGAN: Tell me, Monsieur, how many grains of salt should one put on an egg?

DIAFOIRUS: Oh, six, eight, ten, by even numbers; just as in medications we use odd numbers.

ARGAN: Good day, Monsieur.

Scene 7

BÉLINE: Before I go, little one, I wanted to warn you about something you should keep an eye on. As I passed by Angélique's room, I saw a young man with her, who ran away as soon as he saw me.

ARGAN: A young man with my daughter?

BÉLINE: Yes. Your little daughter Louison was with them. She can tell you the news.

ARGAN: Send her here, love, send her here. Ah, how brazen! Now I'm not surprised by her resistance.

Scene 8

LOUISON: What do you want, papa? My stepmother told me you asked for me.

ARGAN: Yes, come here. Closer. Turn around, raise your eyes, look at me. Ha!

LOUISON: What, papa?

ARGAN: There!

LOUISON: What?

ARGAN: Have you nothing to say to me?

LOUISON: If you like, I can amuse you by telling the story of "Donkey Skin" or the fable of "The Fox and the Crow," that I was taught recently.

ARGAN: That's not what I'm asking.

LOUISON: What, then?

ARGAN: Ah, you sly one! You know very well what I mean.

LOUISON: I'm sorry, papa, I don't.

ARGAN: Is this how you obey me?

LOUISON: What?

ARGAN: Didn't I instruct you that if you see anything, you should come and tell me at once?

LOUISON: Yes, papa.

ARGAN: And have you done it?

LOUISON: Yes, papa. I've come and told you everything I've seen.

ARGAN: And have you seen anything today?

LOUISON: No, papa.

ARGAN: No?

LOUISON: No, papa.

ARGAN: You're sure?

LOUISON: I'm sure.

ARGAN: Well, now! I'll make you see something all right! *(He grabs a handful of switches.)*

LOUISON: Oh, papa!

ARGAN: Ah, you little fraud! You're not telling me you saw a man in your sister's room?

LOUISON: Papa!

ARGAN: This will teach you to lie.

LOUISON: *(Throws herself on her knees)* Oh, papa, forgive me! It's just that my sister told me not to tell you; but I'll tell you everything.

ARGAN: First you'll get whipped for lying. Then we'll see about the rest.

LOUISON: Forgive me, papa!

ARGAN: No, no.

LOUISON: Dear papa, don't whip me!

ARGAN: I will, too.

LOUISON: In God's name, papa, don't do it!

ARGAN: *(Taking hold of her to whip her)* Come on, come on.

LOUISON: Oh, papa, you've hurt me. Look: I'm dead. *(She pretends to be dead.)*

ARGAN: Hold on! What's this now? Louison, Louison! Oh, for God's sake! Louison! Ah, my daughter! Ah, wretched me, my poor daughter's dead. What have I done, miserable fool! Ah, dastardly switches! A plague

on all switches! Ah, my poor daughter, my poor little
Louison!

LOUISON: There, there, papa, don't cry so much. I'm not
all that dead.

ARGAN: See the sly little thing? Oh, well, I'll forgive
you this once, provided you tell me everything.

LOUISON: I will, I will, papa.

ARGAN: Take good care that you do, because here's
a little finger that knows everything; it will tell me if
you're lying.

LOUISON: But, papa, don't tell my sister that I told you.

ARGAN: No, no.

LOUISON: The thing is, papa, that a man came to my
sister's room while I was there.

ARGAN: And?

LOUISON: I asked him what he wanted, and he told me
he was her singing teacher.

ARGAN: Ho, ho! So that's it! And?

LOUISON: Then my sister came.

ARGAN: And?

LOUISON: She said to him: "Get out, get out, get out, my
God! get out, you drive me to despair".

ARGAN: And?

LOUISON: He didn't want to go.

ARGAN: What did he say?

LOUISON: He said all kinds of things.

ARGAN: And what else?

LOUISON: He said this and that, that he really loved her,
that she was the most beautiful girl in the world.

ARGAN: And then what?

LOUISON: And then he knelt down before her.

ARGAN: And then what?

LOUISON: And then he kissed her hands.

ARGAN: And then what?

LOUISON: And then my stepmother came to the door, and he ran away.

ARGAN: There's nothing else?

LOUISON: No, papa.

ARGAN: Hold on, my little finger is mumbling something. *(He puts his little finger to his ear.)* Wait. Eh? Ah, ah, really? Oh-ho, my little finger tells me something you saw and didn't tell me about.

LOUISON: Oh, papa, your little finger is a liar.

ARGAN: Careful, now.

LOUISON: No, papa, don't believe him, he's lying, I promise you.

ARGAN: Well, well, we'll see about that. Go now, and keep an eye out for everything: go! Ah, there are no children anymore. Ah, what a business! I don't even have time to think about my sicknesses. I really can't take any more. *(He collapses in his chair.)*

(Curtain)

END OF ACT TWO

ACT THREE

Scene 1

(Same room)

BÉRALDE: *(Enters)* Well, so, brother, how are you feeling?

ARGAN: Ah, brother, very bad!

BÉRALDE: What do you mean, "very bad"?

ARGAN: Yes, I've gotten so weak, it's unbelievable.

BÉRALDE: That's annoying.

ARGAN: I don't even have strength enough to speak.

BÉRALDE: I've come, brother, to offer you a match for your daughter Angélique.

ARGAN: *(Furious, rising from his chair)* Brother, don't speak to me of that slut. She's cheeky, impertinent, shameless. I'll clap her into a convent before two days go by.

BÉRALDE: Ah, there, that's better! I'm very glad you're getting a little strength back. What do you say we talk?

ARGAN: Excuse me, brother, I'll be back in a minute.

TOINETTE: Here, Monsieur. Don't forget you can't walk without your stick.

ARGAN: Right.

Scene 2

TOINETTE: Please, sir, don't abandon the interests of your niece.

BÉRALDE: I'll do everything to see that she gets what she wants.

TOINETTE: We absolutely must prevent this outrageous marriage he's taken into his head. I've been thinking to myself that it would be a good thing if we could bring in a doctor who suits us, to put him off this Monsieur Purgon and denounce his treatment. But, since we don't have anyone around like that, I've decided to play a little trick of my own.

BÉRALDE: What that?

TOINETTE: A funny little idea. It may turn out luckier than it is wise. Leave it to me. You keep up your side. Here comes our man.

Scene 3

BÉRALDE: Allow me, brother, to ask you not to get yourself all heated up while we talk.

ARGAN: All right, I won't.

BÉRALDE: To reply without any peevishness to whatever I may say to you.

ARGAN: Yes.

BÉRALDE: And to reason together about the matters we have to discuss in a spirit free of all passion.

ARGAN: My God, yes! What a preamble!

BÉRALDE: How is it, brother, that having the fortune you have, and having no other children than a daughter, because I don't count the little one, you talk of putting her in a convent?

ARGAN: How is it, brother, that I'm the master in my family and can do whatever I like?

BÉRALDE: Your wife misses no chance to advise you to get rid of your two daughters, and I don't doubt that, in a spirit of charity, she would be delighted to see them both become nuns.

ARGAN: So, there you go! Right away the poor woman is brought into it; she's the one who does all the harm, and everybody's against her.

BÉRALDE: No, brother, let's leave her out of it. She's a woman who has the best intentions in the world for your family, and is free of any sort of self-interest, who feels a wonderful tenderness for you, and who shows an inconceivable affection and kindness for your children: that is certain. Let's not talk about her, but come back to your daughter. What do you have in mind, brother, in wanting to marry her to a doctor's son?

ARGAN: What I have in mind, brother, is to give myself the sort of son-in-law I need.

BÉRALDE: But that has nothing, brother, to do with your daughter. A more suitable match for her has presented himself.

ARGAN: Yes, but this one, brother, is more suitable for me.

BÉRALDE: But should the husband she takes be for herself, brother, or for you?

ARGAN: He should be, brother, both for her and for me. I want to bring into my family the people I have need of.

BÉRALDE: For the same reason, if your little girl was grown up, you'd marry her to an apothecary?

ARGAN: Why not?

BÉRALDE: Is it possible that you'll stay in bed with your apothecaries and doctors forever, and would want to be sick in spite of all that's human and natural?

ARGAN: What do you mean by that, brother?

BÉRALDE: I mean, brother, that I've never seen a man less sick than you, and I couldn't ask for a better constitution than yours. A great sign that you're well, and that you have a perfectly sound body, is that for all the cures you've taken, you still haven't harmed your good health or dropped dead from all the medicines you've been made to take.

ARGAN: But do you know, brother, that that is what preserves me, and that Monsieur Purgon says I would succumb if he stopped taking care of me for as little as three days?

BÉRALDE: If you're not careful, he'll take such good care of you that he'll send you to the next world.

ARGAN: But let's discuss it a little, brother. So you don't believe in medicine?

BÉRALDE: No, brother, and I see no need to believe in it for the sake of one's well-being.

ARGAN: What? You don't accept the truth of something established all over the world and revered throughout all the ages?

BÉRALDE: Far from accepting the truth of it, I find it, just between us, one of mankind's greatest delusions; and looking at things philosophically, I don't think there's a funnier sort of trumpery. I see nothing more ridiculous than a man who mucks around with curing another man.

ARGAN: Why won't you believe, brother, that a man can cure another?

BÉRALDE: Because, brother, the workings of our
mechanism are still mysteries, which men know
nothing about, and nature has placed veils before our
eyes too thick for us to learn anything about them.

ARGAN: So doctors know nothing, according to you?

BÉRALDE: No, they do, brother. Most of them have a
good knowledge of the humanities, they can speak
beautiful Latin, they can give the Greek names for all
diseases, define them, and classify them; but as for
curing them, they know nothing at all.

ARGAN: But still you must agree that doctors know
more about it than anyone else.

BÉRALDE: They know, brother, what I've told you,
which won't cure much of anything. And all the
excellence of their art consists in a pompous gibberish,
a specious babble, which gives you words instead of
reasons and promises instead of results.

ARGAN: But after all, brother, there are other people as
wise and clever as you; and we see that, when they're
sick, everybody turns to doctors.

BÉRALDE: That's a mark of human weakness, not of the
truth of their art.

ARGAN: But doctors must really believe their art is
genuine, because they use it on themselves.

BÉRALDE: That's because some of them have fallen into
the common error that they profit from, and that others
profit from without falling into it. Your Monsieur
Purgon, for instance, doesn't have any subtlety: he's
all doctor from head to foot; a man who believes
in his rules more than in any mathematical proofs,
and would believe it a crime to think of examining
them; who sees nothing obscure in medicine, nothing
doubtful, nothing difficult, and with impetuous
prejudice, inflexible confidence, crude common-sense

and reasoning, he administers purges and bleedings
at random and without any hesitation. You mustn't
blame him for whatever he may do to you: it's with the
best will in the world that he'll send you out of it, and
in killing you, he'll only do what he's done to his own
wife and children, and if need be would do to himself.

ARGAN: That's because you, brother, have an old
grudge against him. But let's come to the point. What
should you do if you're sick?

BÉRALDE: Nothing, brother.

ARGAN: Nothing?

BÉRALDE: Nothing. All you need to do is rest quietly.
Nature herself, if we let her, will gently get herself out
of the trouble she has fallen into. It's our anxiety, our
impatience, that ruins everything, and almost all men
die of their treatments, not of their diseases.

ARGAN: But you must still agree, brother, that we can
help this nature out in certain ways.

BÉRALDE: My God, brother, these are mere ideas that
we love to feed on. At all times, beautiful fantasies
have insinuated themselves among men, which we
come to believe because they flatter us and it would
be good if they were real. When a doctor speaks to
you of helping, of assisting, of relieving nature, of
removing what harms her and giving her what she
lacks, of restoring her and bringing her back to the
full facility of her functions; when he speaks to you
of rectifying the blood, of soothing the bowels and
the brain, of diminishing the spleen, of restoring the
lungs, of repairing the liver, of fortifying the heart,
of reestablishing and preserving the natural heat,
and of having secrets for extending life over many
long years—he is precisely reciting the romance of
medicine to you. But when it comes down to truth
and experience, you won't find any of that, and it's

the same as with those beautiful dreams which leave you nothing on waking but the annoyance of having believed them.

ARGAN: In other words, all the knowledge in the world is contained in your head, and you claim to know more than all the great doctors of our age.

BÉRALDE: In words and in deeds, they're two different sorts of persons, your great doctors. Hear them talk: they're the cleverest people in the world; see what they do: they're the most ignorant of men.

ARGAN: Oh, yes! You're a great doctor yourself, I see that, and I only wish we had one of those Monsieurs here to rebut your arguments and take you down a peg or two.

BÉRALDE: I, brother, don't take it upon myself to fight against the medical profession; and each of us, at his own peril and hazard, can believe whatever he likes. What I'm saying is just between us. I'd have liked to be able to draw you a little way out of the error you're in and, on that pretext, take you, for your own amusement, to see one of Molière's comedies.

ARGAN: He's an impertinent one, your Molière, with his comedies, and I find it rather ludicrous of him to make fun of honorable men like doctors.

BÉRALDE: It's not doctors he makes fun of, it's the ridiculousness of the profession.

ARGAN: Who is he to go judging the medical profession! It takes a real ninny, a real smart aleck, to mock at consultations and prescriptions, to attack the whole corpus of doctors, and to put such venerable people as these gentlemen on his stage.

BÉRALDE: What do you want him to put there if not the various professions of men? Princes and kings are put there every day, and they're as respectable as doctors.

ARGAN: Damn it to hell, if I were the doctors, I'd take revenge for his impudence! And if he was sick, I'd let him die unattended. Whatever he might say or do, I wouldn't prescribe the least little bleeding, the least little enema for him, and I'd say to him: "Croak! Croak! That'll teach you to make fun of the Medical Faculty next time!"

BÉRALDE: You're really angry with him.

ARGAN: Yes, he's misguided, and if the doctors are smart, they'll do as I say.

BÉRALDE: He'll be even smarter than your doctors, because he'll never ask them for help.

ARGAN: So much the worse for him: he won't get any treatment.

BÉRALDE: He has his reasons for not wanting any. He maintains that it's permissible for vigorous and robust men, who have enough strength to bear the treatment as well as the disease; but that, as for him, he has just strength enough to bear his illness.

ARGAN: What stupid reasons! Listen, brother, let's not talk any more about this man, because it heats my bile, and you'll bring on my illness.

BÉRALDE: I'll gladly stop, brother. And to change the subject, let me tell you that, just because of your daughter's slight resistance, you shouldn't make such a harsh decision as to put her into a convent; that, for the choice of a son-in-law, you should not blindly follow the passion that carries you away, and that, in this matter, you should accommodate yourself a little to your daughter's inclination, since it's for life, and all the happiness of her marriage depends on it.

Scene 4

ARGAN: *(As* FLEURANT *enters, holding a syringe)* Ah, brother, excuse me.

BÉRALDE: What? What are you going to do?

ARGAN: Have that little enema there. It won't take long.

BÉRALDE: You're joking. Can't you go for a minute without enemas and medicines? Put it off for another time, and rest a little.

ARGAN: Make it this evening, Monsieur Fleurant, or tomorrow morning.

FLEURANT: *(To* BÉRALDE*)* What are you butting in for, opposing the prescriptions of medicine, and keeping Monsieur from taking my clyster? Who are you to be so pushy?

BÉRALDE: Go away, Monsieur, it's clear you're not used to addressing faces.

FLEURANT: You shouldn't make light of treatments like that. You're wasting my time. I came here on good instructions, and I shall tell Monsieur Purgon how I was prevented from carrying out his orders and performing my function. You'll see, you'll see…

ARGAN: Brother, you'll be the cause of some disaster.

BÉRALDE: The great disaster of not taking an enema prescribed by Monsieur Purgon. Once again, brother, is there really no way to cure you of the sickness of doctors? Do you want to be buried under their treatments all your life?

ARGAN: My God, brother, you're speaking as a healthy man; but if you were in my place, you'd certainly change your language. It's easy to speak against medicine when you're in perfect health.

BÉRALDE: But what is your sickness?

ARGAN: You'll make me furious! I wish you had my sickness, just to see if you'd go on jabbering like that. Ah, here's Monsieur Purgon!

Scene 5

PURGON: I've just heard some pretty news down there at the door: that my prescriptions are laughed at here, and the treatment I prescribed has been refused.

ARGAN: Monsieur, it's not...

PURGON: That is a rather great effrontery, a strange rebellion of a sick man against his doctor.

TOINETTE: It's appalling.

PURGON: A clyster that I had the pleasure of concocting myself.

ARGAN: It wasn't me...

PURGON: Invented and composed by all the rules of the art.

TOINETTE: He's wrong.

PURGON: And that would have had a marvelous effect on the bowels.

ARGAN: My brother...

PURGON: Rejected with disdain!

ARGAN: It's him...

PURGON: An outrageous act!

TOINETTE: That's true.

PURGON: An enormous offense against the medical profession.

TOINETTE: He's the one...

PURGON: A high crime against the Faculty, which cannot be punished enough.

TOINETTE: You're right.

PURGON: I declare that I am breaking off all dealings with you.

ARGAN: It's my brother...

PURGON: I want no further alliance with you.

TOINETTE: Good for you.

PURGON: And, to end all connection with you, here is the donation I made to my nephew in favor of the marriage. *(He tears up the paper.)*

ARGAN: It's my brother who did all the harm.

PURGON: To despise my clyster!

ARGAN: Bring it here, I'll take it.

PURGON: I would have fixed you up before long.

TOINETTE: He doesn't deserve it.

PURGON: I would have cleaned out your body and emptied it entirely of bad humors.

ARGAN: Ah, my brother!

PURGON: And I wouldn't have needed more than a dozen medicines to empty you out.

TOINETTE: He's unworthy of your care.

PURGON: But since you did not want to be cured at my hands...

ARGAN: It's not my fault.

PURGON: Since you have absconded from the obedience one owes to one's doctor...

TOINETTE: That cries out for vengeance.

PURGON: Since you have declared yourself a rebel against the treatments I have prescribed...

ARGAN: Oh, not at all!

PURGON: I must tell you that I abandon you to your bad constitution, to the intemperance of your bowels, the corruption of your blood, the acidity of your bile, and the feculence of your humors.

TOINETTE: Very well done.

ARGAN: My God!

PURGON: And I'll have you know that in four days' time you'll be in an incurable state.

ARGAN: Oh, mercy!

PURGON: You will fall into bradypepsia.

ARGAN: Monsieur Purgon!

PURGON: From bradypepsia into dyspepsia.

ARGAN: Monsieur Purgon!

PURGON: From dyspepsia into apepsia.

ARGAN: Monsieur Purgon!

PURGON: From apepsia into lientery…

ARGAN: Monsieur Purgon!

PURGON: From lientery into dysentery…

ARGAN: Monsieur Purgon!

PURGON: From dysentery into hydropsy…

ARGAN: Monsieur Purgon!

PURGON: And from hydropsy to the privation of life, which is where your folly will have led you.

Scene 6

ARGAN: Ah, my God, I'm dead! Brother, you've done me in.

BÉRALDE: What? What's the matter?

ARGAN: I can't stand it any more. I already feel the Faculty taking its revenge.

BÉRALDE: Good lord, brother, you're crazy! Not for anything would I want anyone to see you do what you're doing to yourself. Get a hold of yourself, I beg you, come to your senses, and don't let your imagination run away with you.

ARGAN: You see, brother, what strange diseases he threatened me with.

BÉRALDE: Simpleton that you are!

ARGAN: He says I'll become incurable within four days.

BÉRALDE: And what difference does it make what he says? Is he an oracle? It seems to me, listening to you, that Monsieur Purgon holds the thread of your days in his hand, and with supreme authority prolongs it or shortens it as he pleases. Realize that the principles of your life are in you, and that the wrath of Monsieur Purgon is as little capable of making you die as his treatments are of making you live. Here's a chance, if you want it, to cure yourself of doctors, or, if you were born unable to do without them, it's easy enough to find another one, brother, with whom you may run slightly less risk.

ARGAN: Ah, brother, he knows my whole constitution and the way I must be cared for.

BÉRALDE: You're really set in your ways, I can tell you that, and you look at things with strange eyes.

Scene 7

TOINETTE: Monsieur, there's a doctor asking to see you.

ARGAN: What doctor?

TOINETTE: A doctor of doctoring.

ARGAN: I'm asking you who he is.

TOINETTE: I don't know him; but he's as like me as two drops of water, and if I wasn't sure that my mother was an honest woman, I'd say he's some little brother she gave me after my father passed away.

ARGAN: Have him come in.

BÉRALDE: You couldn't do better: one doctor leaves you, another comes along.

ARGAN: I'm really afraid you're going to cause some disaster.

BÉRALDE: Again! Why keep bringing that up?

ARGAN: You see, my mind's full of all those illnesses I know nothing about, those...

Scene 8

TOINETTE: *(Disguised as a doctor)* Allow me to visit you and offer you my small services for all the bleedings and purgings you may be in need of.

ARGAN: Monsieur, I am much obliged to you. By God, it's Toinette herself!

TOINETTE: I beg you to excuse me, Monsieur, I forgot to give my servant an errand. I'll be right back.

ARGAN: Wouldn't you say he really is Toinette?

BÉRALDE: It's true there's a very great resemblance. But it's not the first time this sort of thing has been seen. History is full of such freaks of nature.

ARGAN: Well, as for me, I'm surprised at it, and...

Scene 9

TOINETTE: *(Throwing off her doctor's outfit so quickly that it is hard to believe it was she who appeared as a doctor)* What is it, Monsieur?

ARGAN: How's that?

TOINETTE: Didn't you call me?

ARGAN: Me? No.

TOINETTE: I must be hearing things.

ARGAN: Stay here a little, to see how closely this doctor resembles you.

TOINETTE: *(As she leaves)* No, really, I've got things to do, and I've already seen enough of him.

ARGAN: If I hadn't seen the two of them, I'd believe they were the same.

BÉRALDE: I've read surprising things about these sorts of resemblances, and in our time, too, we've seen cases where everybody was fooled.

ARGAN: Me, I'd have been fooled by this one. I'd have sworn they were the same person.

Scene 10

TOINETTE: *(Disguised as a doctor)* Monsieur, I beg your pardon with all my heart.

ARGAN: It's amazing!

TOINETTE: Please don't take it amiss that I was curious to see such a famous invalid as yourself. Your reputation, which has spread everywhere, may excuse the liberty I have taken.

ARGAN: Monsieur, I am at your service.

TOINETTE: I see, Monsieur, that you keep staring at me. How old do you think I am?

ARGAN: I'd say you might be twenty-six or twenty-seven at the most.

TOINETTE: Ha, ha, ha, ha, ha! I'm ninety.

ARGAN: Ninety?

TOINETTE: Yes. There you see the effect of one of the secrets of my art, which keeps me so fresh and vigorous.

ARGAN: By God, here's a fine young old man of ninety!

TOINETTE: I'm an itinerant doctor, who goes from town to town, from province to province, from kingdom to kingdom, to seek out illustrious materials for my skill, to find invalids worthy of my attention, able to put into practice the great and beautiful secrets I have discovered in medicine. I scorn to amuse myself with the petty hodgepodge of ordinary ailments, with trifling rheumatisms and defluxions, with little fevers, vapors, and migraines. I want important diseases: good continuous fevers with mental delirium, good spotted fevers, good plagues, good mature hydropsies, good pleurisies with inflammations of the chest: that's what I like, that's where I triumph. And I wish, Monsieur, that you had all the diseases I've just named, that you had been given up by all the doctors, desperate, in agony, so that I could show you the excellence of my treatments, and the desire I have to be of service to you.

ARGAN: I am obliged to you, Monsieur, for your kindness.

TOINETTE: Let me feel your pulse. Come on, beat properly. Ahh, I'll make you work the way you should. Ohh, this pulse is playing sassy: I see you don't know me yet. Who is your doctor?

ARGAN: Monsieur Purgon.

TOINETTE: That's a man who hasn't been written down in my list of great doctors. What does he say ails you?

ARGAN: He says it's the liver, and others say it's the spleen.

TOINETTE: They're all ignoramuses. It's the lungs that ail you.

ARGAN: The lungs?

TOINETTE: Yes. What do you feel?

ARGAN: I feel pains in the head now and then.

TOINETTE: Right, it's the lungs.

ARGAN: Sometimes it seems to me there's a veil over my eyes.

TOINETTE: The lungs.

ARGAN: Sometimes I have nausea.

TOINETTE: The lungs.

ARGAN: Sometimes I feel a weariness in all my limbs.

TOINETTE: The lungs.

ARGAN: And occasionally I get pains in the stomach, as if I had colic.

TOINETTE: The lungs. Do you have a good appetite?

ARGAN: Yes, Monsieur.

TOINETTE: The lungs. You like to drink a bit of wine?

ARGAN: Yes, Monsieur.

TOINETTE: The lungs. You get a little sleepy after meals and like to take a nap?

ARGAN: Yes, Monsieur.

TOINETTE: The lungs, the lungs, I tell you. What sort of food does your doctor prescribe for you?

ARGAN: Soup.

TOINETTE: Ignoramus.

ARGAN: Chicken.

TOINETTE: Ignoramus.

ARGAN: Veal.

TOINETTE: Ignoramus.

ARGAN: Bouillon.

TOINETTE: Ignoramus.

ARGAN: Fresh eggs.

TOINETTE: Ignoramus.

ARGAN: And little prunes in the evening to loosen the stomach.

TOINETTE: Ignoramus.

ARGAN: And above all to drink my wine well watered down.

TOINETTE: *Ignorantus, ignoranta, ignorantum.* You should drink your wine pure; and to thicken your blood, which is too thin, you should eat good hearty beef, good hearty pork, good Dutch cheese, gruel and rice, chestnuts and cookies, to stick and conglutinate. Your doctor is a fool. I'll send you one of my own choosing, and I'll come to see you from time to time, while I'm still in this town.

ARGAN: I'm much obliged to you.

TOINETTE: What the deuce is that arm doing on you?

ARGAN: How's that?

TOINETTE: I'd have that arm cut off me right this minute, if I were you.

ARGAN: Why so?

TOINETTE: Don't you see it grabs all the food for itself, and keeps that side from getting anything?

ARGAN: Yes, but I need my arm.

TOINETTE: You've also got a right eye there that I'd have plucked out, if I were in your place.

ARGAN: Pluck out an eye?

TOINETTE: Don't you see it bothers the other one and steals its food? Believe me, have it plucked out as soon as you can, you'll see more clearly with the left eye.

ARGAN: There's no hurry.

TOINETTE: Good-bye. I'm sorry to leave you so soon; but I have to attend a big consultation that's being held about a man who died yesterday.

ARGAN: About a man who died yesterday?

TOINETTE: Yes, to think it over and see what should have been done to cure him. See you soon.

ARGAN: You know that invalids don't show people out.

BÉRALDE: There's a doctor who really seems quite capable.

ARGAN: Yes, but he's a bit too quick about it.

BÉRALDE: All great doctors are like that.

ARGAN: Cut off my arm? Pluck out my eye so that the other one feels better? I'd like it much better if it didn't feel better. A nice operation, to leave me one-eyed and one-armed!

Scene 11

TOINETTE: *(As herself)* Come now, come now, thanks but no thanks, you make me laugh.

ARGAN: What's this?

TOINETTE: Your doctor, by God! He wanted to feel my pulse.

ARGAN: Look at that, and he's all of ninety years old!

BÉRALDE: So, then, brother, since your Monsieur Purgon has just quarreled with you, why don't we talk over the match that's been proposed for my niece?

ARGAN: No, brother, I want to put her in a convent, because she went against my wishes. I see very well that there's some little love affair behind it, and I've found out about a certain secret meeting, which nobody knows I've found out about.

BÉRALDE: Well now, brother, if there should be some small inclination, would that be so criminal, and could it possibly offend you, when it all only leads to such an honorable thing as marriage?

ARGAN: Be that as it may, brother, I'll make a nun of her, that's settled.

BÉRALDE: You're out to please somebody.

ARGAN: I know what you're getting at: you always come back to that. My wife is so dear to your heart!

BÉRALDE: Well, yes, brother, since we're talking open-heartedly, it's your wife I mean. And just as I cannot bear your infatuation for the medical profession, so I cannot bear your infatuation for her, and seeing you walk straight into the traps she sets for you.

TOINETTE: Ah, Monsieur, don't talk about Madame: she's a woman about whom nothing can be said, a woman without guile, and who loves Monsieur, who loves her...you cannot say that.

ARGAN: Just ask her about the caresses she gives me.

TOINETTE: It's true.

ARGAN: How my illness upsets her.

TOINETTE: It really does.

ARGAN: And the cares and troubles she goes to for me.

TOINETTE: That's for sure. Do you want me to convince you and make you see right now how Madame loves Monsieur? *(Aside to* ARGAN*)* Monsieur, allow me to rub his nose in it and show him how wrong he is.

ARGAN: How?

TOINETTE: Madame will be back any minute. Lay yourself out flat in this chair and pretend you're dead. You'll see what grief it causes her when I tell her the news.

ARGAN: All right.

TOINETTE: Only don't leave her in despair too long, because she might just die of it.

ARGAN: Leave it to me.

TOINETTE: *(To* BÉRALDE*)* Hide yourself in that corner there.

ARGAN: Isn't there some risk in pretending to be dead?

TOINETTE: No, no, what risk could there be? Just lay yourself out there. *(Softly)* It will be a pleasure to shame your brother. Here comes Madame. Lie still.

Scene 12

TOINETTE: *(Pretending not to see* BÉLINE, *cries out)* Oh, my God! Ah, how terrible! What a strange thing to happen!

BÉLINE: What is it, Toinette?

TOINETTE: Oh, Madame!

BÉLINE: What's the matter?

TOINETTE: Your husband is dead!

BÉLINE: My husband is dead?

TOINETTE: Alas, yes! The poor deceased has passed away.

BÉLINE: You're sure?

TOINETTE: I'm sure. Nobody knows it's happened yet, and I was quite alone here. He just passed away in my arms. Look, here he is stretched out in this chair.

BÉLINE: Thank heaven! That's a great load off my back. What a fool you are, Toinette, to be upset by his death.

TOINETTE: I thought, Madame, that one ought to weep.

BÉLINE: Come, come, it's not worth the trouble. What kind of loss is it? What good was he on this earth? A man who bothered everybody, dirty, disgusting, some enema or medicine in his belly all the time, forever snorting, coughing, spitting, witless, boring, ill-humored, wearing people out all the time, and scolding the maids and servants day and night.

TOINETTE: There's a nice funeral oration.

BÉLINE: You've got to help me carry out my plan, Toinette, and, believe me, your reward for serving me is assured. Since nobody, fortunately, has been told about it yet, let's carry him to his bed and keep his death hidden until I've finished my business. There are papers, there is money I want to snatch for myself. It's not fair that I spent my best years with him for nothing. Come, Toinette, first let's take all his keys.

ARGAN: *(Sitting up suddenly)* Not so fast.

BÉLINE: *(Surprised and frightened)* Aiee!

ARGAN: So, Madame my wife, this is how you love me!

TOINETTE: Ah, ah, the deceased isn't dead!

ARGAN: *(To* BÉLINE, *as she leaves)* I'm glad I've seen your real fondness for me, and heard the fine eulogy you made over me. There's a little warning that will make me wiser in the future and keep me from doing a lot of things.

BÉRALDE: *(Stepping from his hiding place)* Well, brother, now you know.

TOINETTE: My God, I'd never have believed it! But I hear your daughter. Go back to the way you were, and we'll see how she takes your death. It's not a bad experiment; and while you're at it, you'll find out what feelings your family has for you.

Scene 13

TOINETTE: *(Cries out)* O heavens! Ah, how sad! Oh, unhappy day!

ANGÉLIQUE: What's wrong, Toinette? Why are you crying?

TOINETTE: Alas, I have sad news for you.

ANGÉLIQUE: What is it?

TOINETTE: Your father is dead!

ANGÉLIQUE: You say my father is dead, Toinette?

TOINETTE: Yes. There you see him. He died just now of a weakness that came over him.

ANGÉLIQUE: O heavens! What misery! What a cruel blow! Alas, must I lose my father, all I have left in the world? And, what's more, to add to the despair, must I lose him at a moment when he was angry with me? What will become of wretched me, and what consolation can I find after so great a loss?

Scene 14 and Last

CLÉANTE: What's wrong, my lovely Angélique? What misfortune makes you weep so?

ANGÉLIQUE: Alas, I am weeping for the loss of all that is most dear and precious to me in life: I am weeping for my father's death.

CLÉANTE: O heavens! What a thing to happen! What an unexpected blow! Alas, after the proposal I entreated your uncle to make for me, I was coming to present myself to him, and try by my respects and by my prayers to dispose his heart to grant you to my wishes.

ANGÉLIQUE: Ah, Cléante, let's not talk any more. We must drop all thoughts of marriage. After the loss of my father, I no longer want to be in the world, and I renounce it forever. Yes, father, if I resisted your wishes so much, I will follow at least one of your intentions, and make amends that way for the grief I blame myself for having caused you. Allow me, father, to give you my word here, and to kiss you as a sign of my profound affection.

ARGAN: *(Sits up)* Oh, my daughter!

ANGÉLIQUE: *(Frightened)* Aiee!

ARGAN: Come here. Don't be afraid, I'm not dead. See, you're my flesh and blood, my true daughter; and I'm delighted to have seen your kindness.

ANGÉLIQUE: Ah, what a welcome surprise, father! Since by great good fortune Heaven has returned you to my love, allow me to throw myself at your feet and beg one thing from you. If you are not favorable to my heart's preference, if you refuse me Cléante as my husband, I entreat you at least not to force me to marry another. That is all the favor I ask of you.

CLÉANTE: *(Falls to his knees)* Oh, Monsieur, let yourself be touched by her prayers and by mine, and do not set yourself against the mutual urgings of so fair an affection.

BÉRALDE: Brother, can you still be against it?

TOINETTE: Monsieur, will you be indifferent to so much love?

ARGAN: If he becomes a doctor, I'll consent to the marriage. Yes, become a doctor, and I'll give you my daughter.

CLÉANTE: Very gladly, Monsieur. If that's all it takes to be your son-in-law, I'll become a doctor, even an apothecary, if you like. There's not much to it, and I'd do still more to win the lovely Angélique.

BÉRALDE: But, brother, a thought occurs to me: become a doctor yourself. It will be an even greater convenience to have everything you need in yourself.

TOINETTE: That's true. There's the real way to cure yourself quickly. No illness would dare to toy with the person of a doctor.

ARGAN: I think, brother, that you're making fun of me: am I any age to start studying?

BÉRALDE: Studying, hah! You're smart enough as it is; and there are lots of them who are less clever than you.

ARGAN: But you have to be able to speak good Latin, to know diseases and the necessary treatments for them.

BÉRALDE: When you receive the cap and gown of a doctor, you'll learn all that, and afterwards you'll be cleverer than you might like.

ARGAN: What? When you're dressed like that, you know how to talk about diseases?

BÉRALDE: Yes. You only have to speak in a cap and gown, and all gibberish becomes learned, and all stupidity becomes reasonable.

TOINETTE: Look, Monsieur, your beard alone already counts for a lot: a beard makes more than half a doctor.

CLÉANTE: As for me, I'm ready for anything.

BÉRALDE: Do you want to do it right now?

ARGAN: What do you mean, right now?

BÉRALDE: Just that, and in your own house.

ARGAN: In my own house?

BÉRALDE: Yes. I'm friends with a certain Medical Faculty, who will come right now to perform the ceremony in your living room. It will cost you nothing.

ARGAN: But what do I say, how do I answer?

BÉRALDE: They'll teach you in no time, and they'll write out what you have to say. Go put on some decent clothes, I'll send to fetch them.

ARGAN: All right, let's do it.

CLÉANTE: *(Aside to* BÉRALDE*)* What are you saying? What do you mean by this Faculty of your friends?

TOINETTE: What are you going to do?

BÉRALDE: To entertain us a bit this evening. My friends are actors, and they've made a little interlude out of the reception of a doctor, with dances and music. I want us all to take part in the entertainment, and my brother to play the lead role.

ANGÉLIQUE: But, uncle, it seems to me that you're making a bit too much fun of my father.

BÉRALDE: But, my dear niece, it's not making fun of him so much as following his own fancies. This is all just between us. Each of us can take a part, and we'll play the comedy for one another. Carnival permits it. Come quickly and get everything ready.

CLÉANTE: *(To* ANGÉLIQUE*)* You agree to it?

ANGÉLIQUE: Yes, since my uncle leads the way.

END OF ACT THREE

RECEPTION INTO THE FACULTY OF MEDICINE

(Several decorators come to prepare the room and place the benches in rows, after which the whole company, made up of eight SYRINGE-BEARERS, *six* APOTHECARIES, *twenty-two* DOCTORS, *the man to be received as a doctor, eight dancing and two singing* SURGEONS, *enters and takes its places according to rank.)*

PRESIDENT:
> Knowledgissimi doctores,
> Medicini professores,
> You who hic assembled estis,
> And you other Messiores,
> Most fidel executores
> Of the facultatis judgments,

Surgeóni ánd apéthecári,
> And tota compania, to you
> Health, honor, pots of money,
> And bonum appetitum, too.

> My learned confreri, I cannot
> But admirari to myself
> That excellent inventio,
> The medical professio.

Such a bella cosa, and such a lucky find,
> Is this blessed medicina,
> That it's nomine alone,
> Astonishing miraculo,

Since a lungo time ago
Has allowed so many men
Of omne sort to live à gogo.

Per totam terram we can see
The grandam vogam that is we,
And how grandes and petiti
Are with us infatuati.
Tótus múndum, séeking our remédios,
Looks upon us sicut Deos;
And to our prescriptiones
We sée submíssos kíngs and príncipes.

Dunque it makes for nostrae sapientiae,
Boni sensus and prudentiae,
That we continue to travaillare
So as to better conservare
Ourselves in such credito, voga, et honore,
And prendere gardam that we recevere
In our learned corpore
Only personas capabiles,
And totas dignas to fulfill
Their functions honorabiles.

That is why you are now convocati:
And I believe you will find
Worthy materiam medici
In the savanti homine you here see,
Who in all things omnibus
I give you ad interrogandum
And deeply examinandum
In your capacitatibus.

FIRST DOCTOR:
Since mihi permitam Domine Presidentus,
And all these docti Doctores,
And participants illustres,
Most savanti Bacheliero,
Whom estimo et honoro,

I ásk you the cáusam et ratiónem why
    Opium induces sleep?

BACHELOR:
    The docto Doctore has asked me
What is the causam et rationem why
    Opium induces sleep,
        To which I reply
    That it contains
    A sleep-inducing virtus
    Of which the natura
    Is to dull the sensus.

CHORUS:
Bene, bene, bene, bene respondere:
    Dignus is he to entrare
    In our learned corpore.

SECOND DOCTOR:
With the permission of Domine Presidentus,
    The most learned Facultatis,
    And all the compania
    Partaking of this sessione,
I ask of you, most learned Bacheliere,
    In the maladia
    Called hydropisia,
    What are the remedia
    That ought to be applied?

BACHELOR:
First clysterium donare,
    Then seignare,
    Then purgare.

CHORUS:
Bene, bene, bene, bene respondere:
    Dignus is he to entrare
    In our learned corpore.

THIRD DOCTOR:
If it seems good to Domine Presidentus,

The most learned Facultati,
And the present compania,
I ask of you, most learned Bacheliere,
        In cases of eticis,
    Pulmonicis and asmaticis,
    Which remedia you find proper.

BACHELOR:
First clysterium donare,
    Then seignare,
    Then purgare.

CHORUS:
Bene, bene, bene, bene respondere:
    Dignus is he to entrare
    In our learned corpore.

FOURTH DOCTOR:
    Upon these maladias
The learned Bacheliere has spoken maravillas,
But if I do not weary Domine Presidentus,
    The learned Facultatem,
    And all the honorabilem
    Companiam of listeners,
I would put to him unam questionem.
    Yesterday a maladus
    Fell into my manus:
He had a grandam feveram with fluctuationem,
    Grandam dolorem of the head,
    And grandum malorum in the side,
    With granda difficultate
    And paina de respirare:
        Kindly tell me,
        Learned Bacheliere,
        What to do for him?

BACHELOR:
First clysterium donare,

Then seignare,
Then purgare.

FIFTH DOCTOR:
But if the maladia
Is opiniatria
And will not go away,
What to do for him?

BACHELOR:
First clysterium donare,
Then seignare,
Then purgare.

CHORUS:
Bene, bene, bene, bene respondere:
Dignus is he to entrare
In our learned corpore.

PRESIDENT:
Do you swear to keep the statutes
Praescripta by the Facultatem
With sensu and judgemento?

Bachelor
I swear.

PRESIDENT:
And in omnibus
Consultationibus
To follow the old opinion
Whether it's good or bad.

BACHELOR
I swear.

PRESIDENT:
And never to make use
Of any remidiis
Except those of the learned Facultatis,
Even if the maladus
Should collapse and die.

BACHELOR:
>I swear.

PRESIDENT:
>I now with this learned
>And venerable boneto
>Do give and grant to you
>The virtue and the power
>>To medicate,
>>Purgate,
>>Bleedate,
>>Pierceate,
>>Inciseate,
>>Amputate,
>>And terminate
>With impunity the world over.

(All the SURGEONS *and* APOTHECARIES *come in step to bow down before him.)*

BACHELOR
>Great doctors of the doctrine
>Of rhubarb and of senna,
No doubta for mea it would be a foolish thinga,
>Inepta and ridicula,
>If I wentam so farra
>As to sing your praisum,
And attempted to addendum
>Lights to the bright sunello,
>And starums to the sky-o,
>Waves to the Oceanus,
>And rosas to the springum.
Accept that with a singularum wordo,
>For toto gratitudino,
I render thanks unto your learned corpore.
>To you, to you I owe
Much more than to natura and to pater mio:
>Natura and pater mio
>A hominem have made me,

But you, which is much more,
Have made of me a doctor.
Honor, favor, and gratia
Here, in this very cardia,
Have imprinted sentimenta
That will endure forever.

CHORUS
Vivat, vivat, vivat, vivat a hundred times vivat,
    Novus Doctor, who parlays so well!
For a thousand, thousand years may you eat and drink,
    And bleed and kill!

(All the SURGEONS *and* APOTHECARIES *dance to the music
of instruments and voices, the clapping of hands and the
rapping of the* APOTHECARIES' *mortars.)*

A SURGEON:
    May he live to see
    His learned prescriptiones
    Fill all the boutiquas
    Of the surgeorum
    And apothiquarum!

CHORUS:
Vivat, vivat, vivat, vivat a hundred times vivat,
    Novus Doctor, who parlays so well!
For a thousand, thousand years may you eat and drink,
    And bleed and kill!

ANOTHER SURGEON:
    May all the anni
    For him be boni
    And favorabiles,
    And let there be nothing
    But pestas, verolas,
    Feveras, pleuresias,
    Flows of blood and dysenterias!

CHORUS:
Vivat, vivat, vivat, vivat a hundred times vivat,

Novus Doctor, who parlays so well!
For a thousand, thousand years may you eat and drink,
  And bleed and kill!

(Curtain)

END OF PLAY

Made in the USA
Monee, IL
03 March 2023

29118999R00049